AF480043

THE INCREDIBLE WORLD OF PLANTS

Cool Facts You Need to Know
Nature for Kids
Children's Nature Books

Speedy Publishing LLC

40 E. Main St. #1156

Newark, DE 19711

www.speedypublishing.com

Copyright 2018

All Rights reserved. No part of this book may be reproduced or used in any way or form or by any means whether electronic or mechanical, this means that you cannot record or photocopy any material ideas or tips that are provided in this book.

In this book, we're going to talk about the incredible world of plants. So, let's get right to it! If you were walking on Earth, 150 million years ago, you would notice something very unusual. Everything would look green and there would be lots of plants, especially different types of ferns, but you wouldn't see any flowers. That's because on the evolutionary scale flowering plants are fairly recent. They began to evolve about 140 million years ago and started thriving right away.

Flowers are the reproductive parts of plants, but not all plants have flowers. Non-flowering plants, the type that evolved on Earth to begin with, sometimes reproduce using spores and sometimes they use seeds.

CATEGORIES OF PLANTS

There are two major categories of plants—non-flowering and flowering. Within the non-flowering there are two categories, the type that produces spores and the type that produces seeds.

NON-FLOWERING PLANTS THAT PRODUCE SPORES

Mosses and ferns are some of the oldest plant types on Earth. Scientists believe that some fern species have been on Earth for more than 350 million years. These types of non-flowering plants produce spores in order to reproduce. To make sure that some new plants thrive, these plants have evolved to produce huge numbers of spores.

fern and moss

spore moss on a tree

The spores are single-celled and are very lightweight, so the wind carries them. When the wind dies down, it drops them in new locations where the tiny spores could eventually grow to become full-grown plants. Unlike other plants that require male and female parts, a non-flowering plant with spores uses its spores to reproduce and doesn't have male or female parts.

MOSSES

Mosses are plants that don't have root systems. They attach to rocks or soil with special growths that are named rhizoids. Soft and rather spongy, mosses usually grow to a height of just a few inches. They grow clumped together in areas that are shady and damp. Mosses reproduce using spores instead of flowers or seeds. Mosses have thrived on Earth since millions of years ago and these primitive plants are still thriving. Scientists have categorized over 12,000 species.

green moss

fern

FERNS

Ferns have stems and roots so they are more complicated plants than mosses. Their leaves are known as fronds. Underneath these fronds, they produce the casings for spores. These casings just look like brown spots. When the spots dry out, the spores travel into the air until they are deposited on the ground a distance away where they can start new plants.

NON-FLOWERING PLANTS THAT PRODUCE SEEDS

Not all non-flowering plants produce spores, some produce "naked seeds," which simply means that their seeds have no hard covering like the seeds of plants that have flowers. The seed of a gymnosperm is exposed to the air. In fact, the word "gymnosperm" actually means "naked seeds." Types of gymnosperms include:

Cycads, which look like ferns or palm trees but are neither one.

cycad tree

Conifer trees, which typically grow in the forest—these include pine trees, redwood trees, spruce trees, cypress trees, cedar trees, and junipers—and all have cones.

Ginkgo plants, which are also called "maidenhair trees,"
and thrive even in polluted environments.

conifer trees

The conifers are the major group of gymnosperms. "Conifers" comes from the words that mean "having or bearing cones." If you've ever looked closely at these types of trees you would notice that their "leaves" are like needles. These needles are very sturdy and don't dry out easily. They are designed so the trees or plants can thrive in cold climates that are also windy and dry.

The woody trees in this category use cones to produce their soft seeds. The cone acts as a way to protect the seeds until they are ready to be released. Conifers have male and female cones. The job of the male cones is to produce and release pollen. The released pollen floats on the wind and if it lands on a female cone, then that particular cone will be fertilized and produce seeds. Even though the seeds are naked, they are protected by the hard shell of the cone until they are ready to float away.

pine cone in tree

The seeds of the conifer are really amazing. These seeds have wings of their own! When the female cone releases them, they will glide upon the wind until they reach a new patch of ground. If the ground is rich with nutrients, they will begin to germinate and eventually to grow.

FLOWERING PLANTS PRODUCE SEEDS

Flowering plants are vascular plants. Vascular plants have tubular tissues that carry water and minerals throughout the plant. The name that scientists use for flowering plants is angiosperm, which comes from the Greek words for "vessel" and "seed."

LIFE-CYCLE OF ANGIOSPERMS

All angiosperms go through a cycle as they develop from seeds, grow, and then reproduce.

hibiscus stamens

SEEDS

All angiosperms begin their lives as tiny seeds. The seeds have a shell that is hard. This shell is designed to protect the embryo of the seed that is inside. If you open up a seed, you'll see the embryo of the baby plant.

GERMINATION

The seed is deposited on the ground. There are many different ways that this can happen. One way is if a bird eats a fruit that has seeds and then poops them out on the ground. Another way is if you buy a packet of seeds and plant them yourself. Still another way is if the fruit drops off the plant and subsequently decays.

seed germination

stages of germination

Some seeds will be placed in areas where they can't grow. However, if the right conditions exist they will start to grow, which is called the process of germination. The seed will need water, nourishing soil, and fresh air in order to germinate. Once it starts, it will put out some tiny roots and then it will grow stems.

SPROUTS OR SEEDLINGS

The growth of the seed usually takes place under the ground until it eventually pushes through the soil. When it gets above the soil, it's called a sprout or a seedling.

group of green sprouts

ADULT PLANT

The seedling will continue to grow until it becomes an adult plant. It will have stems, a complete root system, and leaves.

REPRODUCTIVE STAGE

Next, the adult plant will flower. The flower is the reproductive part of the plant. Sometimes the flower has both male and female parts. Sometimes it only contains the female part of the plant.

flowering plant

THE FLOWER STRUCTURE

A flower is an amazing structure. It has so many parts that work together to create the seeds needed for reproduction. Here are the major parts of a flower:

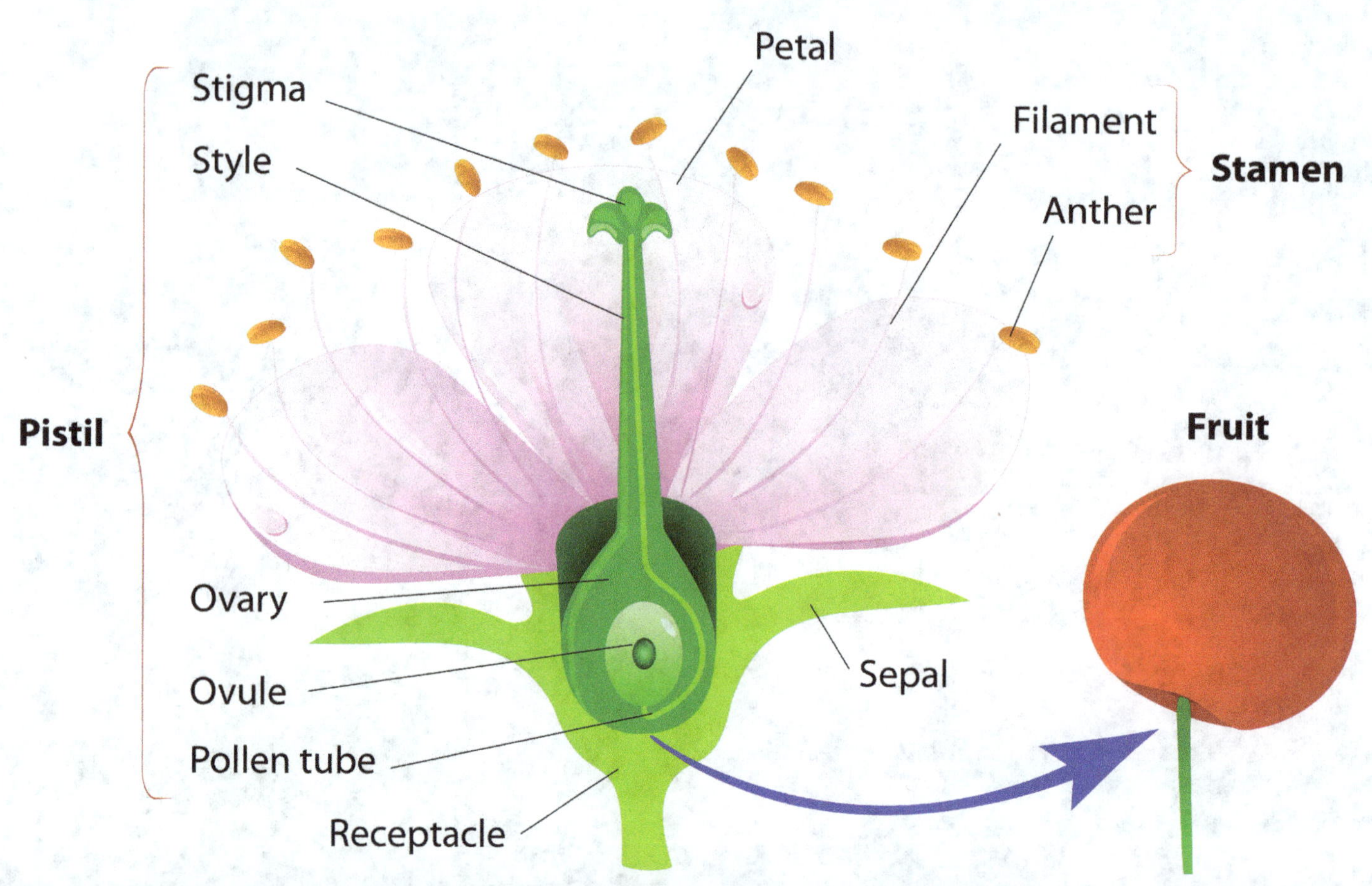

SEPAL

This part of the flower holds up and protects the flower's petals. The structure of all the sepals that are joined together is known as the calyx.

sepals and peduncle of a yellow rose

PETAL

Most flowers are very colorful. Their individual pieces, which look something like leaves, are called petals. Scientists believe that the petals of flowers originally evolved from leaves. The colorful petals attract insects and birds that are needed for the process of pollination.

STAMEN

The stamen is the male part of the plant. You can remember that information if you notice that the word stamen has "men" in it. The stamen creates pollen. The stamen has two parts: the filament and the piece on the top called the anther.

ANTHER

The anther has lobes that hold sacs of pollen.

FILAMENT

The filament is a stalk. It attaches the anther to the rest of the flower.

PISTIL

The flower's female part is the pistil. The pistil is composed of the carpel as well as the stigma.

STIGMA

The stigma is the sticky piece that collects the pollen.

CARPEL

The carpel is the flower's ovary. It holds ovules that if pollinated will become seeds.

FRUIT

Once a flower is fertilized, the ovules in its carpel will change into seeds and the flower will transform and become a fruit.

SEED

The seed is the beginning of a new plant. Seeds come in all different shapes and sizes depending on their parent plants. Inside a seed is the tiny embryo of the plant, some food for it, and an outside seed coat that protects it until it's time for it to germinate.

planting seed in soil

POLLINATION

Pollination is a fascinating process. In order for the ovules to become seeds they have to receive pollen. Birds as well as insects play a role in getting the pollen from one spot to another. For example, a hummingbird sticks its tongue into a flower to drink some nectar. Some of the pollen gets stuck on the hummingbird while it's drinking. When the hummingbird goes to the next flower, the pollen that it carried with it from the other flower brushes off onto the stigma of the second flower. Then it drops down into the carpel to fertilize the ovule.

THE SMELL OF FLOWERS

In addition to attracting insects and birds with their beautiful petals and sweet nectar, flowers usually give off a beautiful scent. However, not all flowers emit good smells. The largest flower in the world gives off a smell of dung!

Rafflesia - the largest flower in the world

SUMMARY

There are many different types of plants on Earth. Two major categories of plants are non-flowering and flowering. Some types of non-flowering plants use spores to reproduce and others use seeds. Flowering plants have male and female parts. They are called angiosperms and they produce fruit that contains seeds in order to reproduce.

Awesome! Now that you know about the two major types of plants, you can read more interesting information about plants in Baby Professor books like Flowering vs. Non-Flowering Plants: Knowing the Difference.

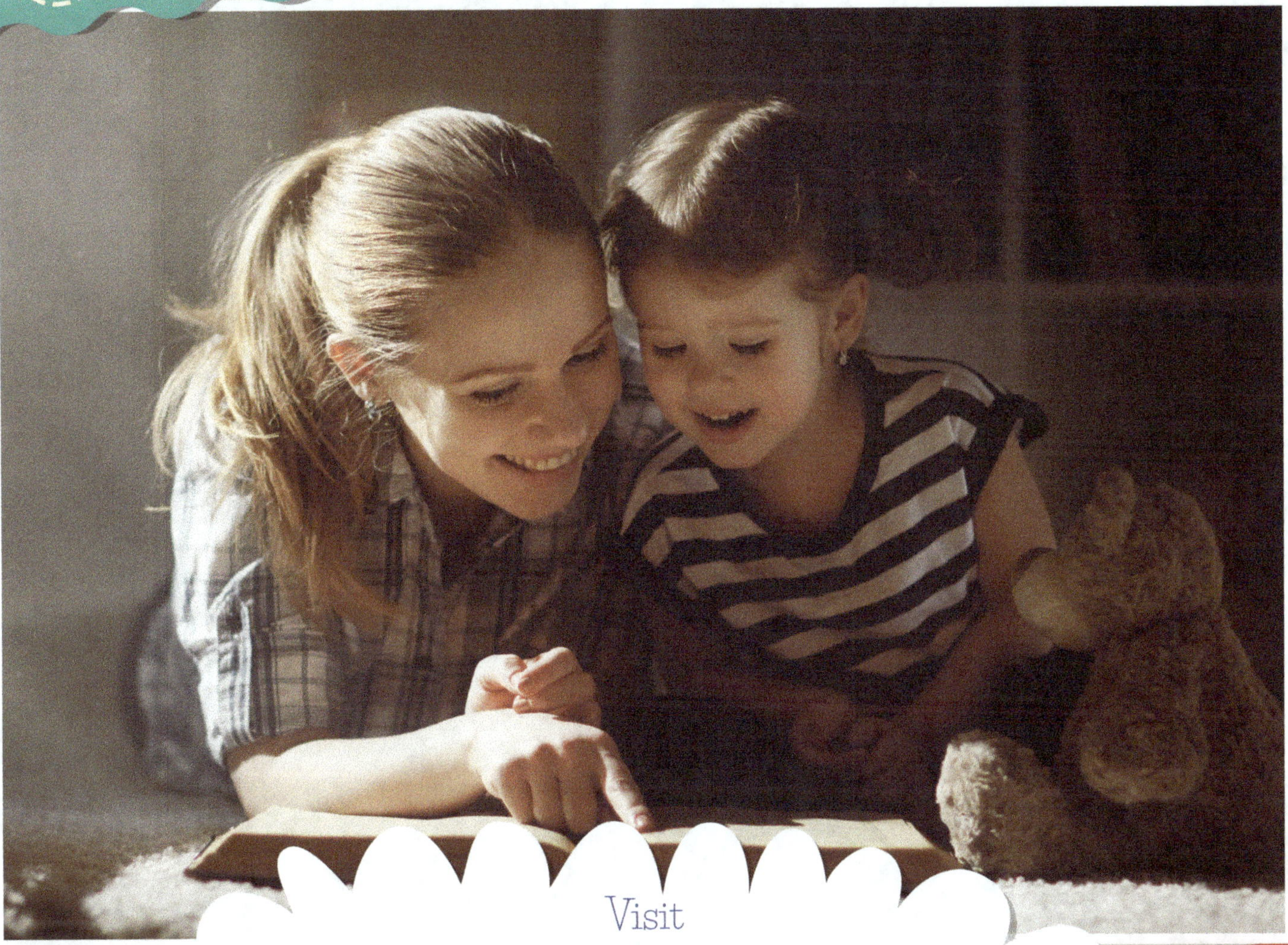

Visit

www.BabyProfessorBooks.com
to download Free Baby Professor eBooks
and view our catalog of new and exciting
Children's Books

www.ingramcontent.com/pod-product-compliance
Lightning Source LLC
Chambersburg PA
CBHW060226120726
48009CB00003B/170